For Jack and Norah,
George and Nellie
thank you

Books by Steven Flint -
The Sun And The Boy
Lev Loveheart
Twenty one collections of Haiku poetry

Cover image by Wendy Tobin
@twendi66 instagram

Copyright Steven Flint 2024
All rights reserved

Until You Return

Hidden qualities
like light that makes a rainbow
you reveal your depths

A verse from nature
words written in morning dew
the ink of the soul

Contents of the heart
poignant lines of poetry
strewn across the page

Synonym for love,
I didn't find another word
that means what you mean

I feel like Sunday
spirited and plentiful
fattened on sunshine

First April shower
warm raindrops washing over
the season's blossom

Children out playing
filling the air with the sound
of their spring voices

I only wonder
did you dream about me when
I dreamt about you

Looking for today
morning mist at the window
things I must decide

Who are we kidding?
It's clear we are two ends of
the same piece of string

I sleep, I travel
to the past to the future
I visit my life

Time ticks in neutral
early morning, random thoughts
thinking not thinking

The heart desires love
and love requires a poem,
beauty of our needs

Once a biscuit tin
now a box of memories,
keeping life's sweet taste

April, early dawn
a single bird in full voice
praising the daylight

Girl with yoga mat
a textbook figure of health
perfection of Om

Letters and poems
love in the old fashioned way
harmony of words

Kingdom or empire?
Shallow men build their glory
on the sands of time

Stronger than moonlight
sharper than a laser beam
the soul foils the dark

Whispering folklore
the olden voice of the moon
lulls us into dreams

Admire the sunrise
every strand of gold woven
in its royal robe

Houdini and a
butterfly release themselves
from a straight jacket

Every tree they fell
every ocean they pollute
every soul they sell

I hear a bird sing
outside in the spring blossom
his song strong and clear

Looking for the moon
I see a faint white crescent
in the twilight haze

Another darkness,
watching the stars made by men
bleak constellation

Shadow of the crow
swoops down on the pigeon's nest
swallows all the eggs

Cameo poet,
catching the moment with his
brief observations

Until you return
the sky will be heartache blue
yellow ribbon sun

How close can you get
before the flame starts to burn?
Love has no answer

Books make great presents
notably poetry books.
Words, the timeless gift

Build me a tree house
between the boughs of the oak
a home to dream in

Passion of April,
the bees are making honey
fledglings learn to fly

Spaces between words
the things we forget to tell,
a prudent silence

Promise of heaven
I want to see the glory
hidden from my eyes

I find you again
in a song, in a poem
always on repeat

In the morning breeze
a dandelion floating
carelessly away

Another weekend
the parks are full, seaside too
sharing the sunshine

Teenager in love
overpowered by the heart
he knows what it is

Saving up the nights
April moon draped in silver
coins we dream to spend

Echo in the sea
I hear your voice like soft waves,
calling of the soul

It's only one life,
from everything it could be
let it be your truth

Laughter of sunlight
filling the windows, bringing
felicity home

Morning miracle
born from a ray of sunlight
world without limit

Seeking urgently
the ethereal nature
hidden in the world

You showed up today,
took the time and did your best,
you made the effort

Single malt whiskey
it leaves many nuances
of fire in the throat

View from my window
watching the gentle moonlight
of a spring evening

Seven nights a week
a flame burns through the darkness
the will of the soul

Like an uncut cake
dawn pending in calm silence
the street lights shut off

A beautiful life
endeavour and commitment,
it's in the making

Dew hangs in the air
not yet the first ray of light
a dozen bird songs

Without you, I am
a half built house, a lost ring
a song with no tune

Spring inspiration
poem written in lilac
jacaranda words

Sunny afternoon,
'PERFECT' printed on your shirt,
I couldn't agree more

Everything is cool,
May arranges her flowers
the weekend arrives

Throwing away stones
never knowing they were the
diamonds worth keeping

The sun in slow descent
a kite flying in the wind
schoolboy horizons

Dreamy existence
voyager under moonlight
tomorrow whispers

Things that should have been
things that should never have been,
the strange path of fate

Love without wanting,
it's a dream we all dream of
human fulfillment

While tomorrow waits
and yesterday drifts away
mold the here and now

Love is a notebook
page after page of blank sheets
waiting to be filled

Kestrel hovering
balancing on a hair's breadth
between flight and swoop

Secret disclosure
blue is the colour of love
your eyes tell me so

Drawn into your gaze
invitation without words
the petal of your soul

An old prophecy
chronicled by a wise soul
Love will persevere

Written in the moon
a poem in neon light
words to guide the heart

Belonging to love
to be held, not beholden,
passport to the world

Common as raindrops
small miracles fill our days
the priceless wonder

May writes her verse in
the poetry of seasons
gentle wildflower

Ballerina shoes
light like the wings of a swan
flying to the lake

An enduring Truth
nothing is lost forever,
the precious return

An awkward silence
much like an ill fitting shoe
uncomfortable

Blunt words carry weight
sharp clarity of meaning,
poetic knockouts

Wherever I go
I carry my history
I carry my dreams

Old soul, means wise heart
sees itself in another,
soothes the storm with love

For a new born child
you choose a name, for this life
you choose a meaning

Perfection of blue
tranquil waters hug the shore
dreams from the seafront

Seeing each other,
sea blue sky a sky blue sea
interconnected

Witnessing beauty
the charm of a brown eyed girl
confirms my belief

From seed to sapling
from branch to leaf, trunk to twig,
complex like a man

I opened a door
that led to a door to what
I was looking for

The walls I couldn't climb
stars I never reached, the dreams
I still hold on to

These uncertain times
everything held together
by a strand of hope

Gently breathing in
hold your breath, feel life, exhale
release the worry

Drawn by your presence
silent sophistication
permeates the air

Words with soft edges
I choose the best to write a
poem about you

No moon overhead
night darker than usual
words not yet written

Abandoned body,
your mind lost in a dream world
somewhere far away

Corner shop dreamer
Nurse Gladys Emmanuel
just beyond his reach

Octaves in the wind
high pitched notes blow through the night
learning nature's flute

My mind in a whirl
remembering, forgetting
missing the birdsong

Sitting quietly
our longest conversation
watching the sunset

For the ship that sailed,
for the love that slipped away,
something takes its place

Days following days
the sun bestows riches from
its fortune of gold

Still awake at night
resting in each other's arms
thinking our silence

We hazard magic
splinters of our souls reveal
a latent power

The May sky chooses
a light shade of blue from its
drawer of colours

On the highway south
passing eucalyptus trees
in spangled twilight

Sea, porcelain blue
water clear as the daylight
still a little cold

With bucket and spade
her first photo by the sea
meeting the water

Promises we keep
lettered deep in a gold ring
kept on a finger

Many shoes she keeps
in cupboards in drawers in
rows under the bed

Floundering alone
we seek their hand in darkness
the touch of safety

Enter the dragon
courage power and control
Bruce Lee in haiku

Winter without love
life is a lonely affair
embraced by the cold

Poem from the night
as you sleep, I leave a word
under your pillow

Petals have fallen
all the colours of June blow
softly in the wind

For our sleeplessness
the night offers a new moon
time to try again

A lucky horseshoe
I'll hang it over the door,
not that I believe

A blade of green grass
vital and precise like a
line of poetry

At the water's edge
a moment to contemplate
life's tranquility

Old mythology
about dragons and mermaids
capturing new hearts

Fractions of seconds
moments within a moment,
knowing the divine

Love blooms like summer
spreads unequivocally
encompassing all

Of my own design,
the things I wanted to be
when I was a boy

Words that come to heal
poem for a broken heart
balsam for the soul

The fighter inside
is not the violent type
but a survivor

Given to fever
my temperature rises
when you are around

A glass of water,
it looks much different in
the height of summer

Her pink bikini
appears all the more vibrant
against her brown skin

A lyrical moon
whispering beauty into
the heart of midnight

Every battle scars,
another generation
makes the same mistakes

Psalm for the evening
prayers and benedictions
for a lover's soul

Now, is not a dream
Now, is the wakefulness of
a jubilant soul

Another bird song
articles of poetry
I store in your heart

Nature heals itself
rises out of the ashes
stronger than before

A summer daydream
walking barefoot through the fields
minding the daisies

Paisley patterned sky
white tear shaped clouds swirling in
the mesmeric blue

An eternal love
carved in the bark of a tree
growing through the years

Poem for the muse
new words are born in your eyes
I capture a smile

Rolling Stones t-shirt
tight fitting jeans, cool and chic
born to rock and roll

The voice of the rose
red is the colour of night
when you sing your song

Daylight robbery
a stranger can steal your heart
no crime committed

Written in the heart
gentle and stormy poems
seasons and stories

A man without roots,
drifting like a fallen leaf
never knowing home

Feline reasoning
purr for a saucer of milk
meow for some love

You smudge your lipstick
not to attract attention
but warn pretenders

A poem for you
words my heart laboured to say
silent they remain

The more they fix it
the more it gets broken, their
politics of doom

Effigy of smoke
a crow flies out of the flames
black wings mar the sky

The echoes we hear
friends we lost along the way
calling to our hearts

Free to imagine
summer sky delicate blue
the dreams left to dream

Window half open
sometimes letting out the warmth
letting in the cold

Your gentle breathing
writes poetry in my soul
nothing left unread

A heart that breaks is
a heart that loves, there is no
weakness in caring

Tastes like June twilight
under the strawberry leaf
the fruit of summer

Poems are milestones
they mark one's growth and record
new understandings

A well polished moon
so bright I can see a face
in its silver light

The art of living,
an animated poem
properly sublime

The time it takes to
bake a cake, grow a flower
all divine moments

July proposal
centigrade of happiness
mercury will burn

Without a blemish
perfect to the last moment
apricot sunset

Visions of turquoise,
the enchanting sea makes me
believe in mermaids

Nature's perfection
originally bottled
in a drop of dew

The myna bird sings,
from his little yellow beak
a beautiful song

I try to access
that magic silence from which
all music is born

Like a summer breeze
words of the poem blow life
through the longing soul

Furious in love
the senses long to drown in
the storm of passion

Of many beauties
this singular world is made,
every craft an art

If love will have us,
two penniless guests at its
luxury hotel

Harmony of flight
the soul follows the light of
many horizons

The summer moon
writes poetry through the night
the words to my dreams

I hold on to you
like I hold a kite, amazed
afraid to let go

Garden of flowers,
June July and August all
blossom in your soul

Endearing July
kindness pours out of the sun
healing our darkness

In the school of life
lessons are free and varied
you live and you learn

My heart is hungry
knocks on the walls of my chest
calling for manna

I'll always want you
so hold me now forever
even when we part

Self made millionaire
its not the cash in the bank,
but love in the heart

On close inspection,
reading the lines in your hand
I find good tidings

Slender moon tonight,
gentle in its appearance
a breath of haiku

Charity of heart
like seeds of a sunflower
you share your kindness

With earth in our bones
and sea pulsing through our veins
we shine like night stars

Working through the stress
learning to unknot tension
regaining balance

Rising from darkness
faithful warrior of peace
the sun waves her flag

Milton Keynes UK
Ingram Content Group UK Ltd.
UKHW020744051024
449151UK00011B/413